IWork for ME

7 Steps for Successful Entrepreneurship

Snehal R. Singh

DEDICATION

Have you ever had a book dedicated to You?

No?

Let's Fix that

This Book is dedicated to

....

GRATITUDE

"**G**ive **thanks** to the **LORD**, for he is good; his love endures forever." Psalm 107:1

Love begins with me. This book is a journey of 2 years penned down. In this journey, I have learnt that the strongest person I know is Me. I have learnt to Love Myself first. It makes me strong and able to share love with the world.

Love begins at home. For me that means Raj, my very loving and supportive husband. I am blessed and grateful.

I am indebted to Divya who has held me accountable and made sure the book is out this year.

I am grateful to my editor Vimala Vadivale who has been very kind and worked on extreme timelines with me.

I am very grateful to Daniel Joseph who helped me with this book.

I am grateful to my 7-year-old friend Thaanya who motivates me everyday to write. Her cute questions – "Snehal Aunty you are an author, right? What is your next book about?" push me out of my comfort zones and procrastination. Thank you Thaanya for all the love and respect.

I am grateful to my sister Pooja. She's really been my rock. I thank God for giving me selfless parents – who have just given me and never asked anything in return. I love you Aai and Pappa

Last and most important, I want to thank is You – My readers. I am indebted to the overwhelming love and respect I received with my first 2 books and all work I have done so far. Thank you.

Table of Contents

FOREWORD BY
MATT GAGNON

There are many people out there who are built to thrive within the walls of the corporate world. Then there are those courageous few who choose to take the plunge into the exciting world of entrepreneurship with the opportunity of being their own boss calling and being in charge of their own destiny.

The story that is not often told about entrepreneurship or working from home is the need for personalized structures, systems, and behaviors in order to truly thrive.

I instantly connected with Snehal's testimony in "I Work for Me", as it perfectly articulates the raw honest journey of entrepreneurship. Entrepreneurship can be thrilling and also incredibly overwhelming. Snehal does a brilliant job of creating a series of clear simple steps that will set up any entrepreneur for success. This is the perfect guide for any entrepreneur, whether new or experienced.

Matt Gagnon, CPCC, PCC, FOP
The Lion || Mindset Coach || Epic Storyteller || Keynote Speaker || Forbes Council || Best Selling Author || Rule Breaker || Family || Bulletproof Optimist || 1Samuel17:48

LinkedIn - https://www.linkedin.com/in/mattgagnon1/

INTRODUCTION

I have been in business for the last eight years. Though this may sound ordinary, it is an achievement for me, with a story behind it. I come from a family background of 'conservative' people who strongly believed in working for others, being employed and having an employer. You worked within a set framework, you 'obeyed' your boss, you rose in the hierarchy....and you retired.

Having always been the black sheep of the family, I stepped out to do something different; I decided to have my own business. Although, like my family, I started with being employed, I quickly moved into freelancing, and soon started on my own.

As you can imagine, it was challenging, considering that I had no one in the family who had experience in having their own business, no one to go to for advice, no one to ask when in doubt, and no one I could run things through to know if I was on the right track.....but those were not the only challenges I had.

My life was not like that of the everyday person, and it also proved to be a challenge in another form. My education was not done in the conventional style, as I officially only went through to the twelfth grade.

What this meant was that despite my certifications and training, I still lacked confidence in my capabilities to run a business. I felt that my inadequacy, when it came to having some background in business, would affect me...and it did. So my fears and doubts grew with each opportunity they found.

I believed many negative thoughts. I believed I was not qualified enough, I believed I was too young to be a leader, I believed no one was going to listen to me, and before long these thought patterns were impeding my growth. The walls grew so tall and soon they were standing between me and success, and feeling suffocated, I knew I had to do something to break free and rise.

I Work For Me is a book which serves as a guide, showing how I worked with myself so I could serve others. This book shows you how I chose me; it shows my journey with me...to me, which helped me overcome those feelings of inadequacy, so I could rise to help and serve the world. This book shows how I realized I.M.B.R.A.N.D.

As Iyanla Vanzant said, "it is not selfish to put yourself first, it is self-full. You must be good to yourself first if you want to be of service in life." I Work For Me shows the entrepreneur, the life coach, the freelancer, the professional, the one who works from home, the solo-preneur, no matter your gender or uniqueness, how to relate well with self and work, and how to merge the relationships in a beautiful way. It shows how to effectively be a brand.

Notice I didn't say your job, or your job title, I said your work, and your work is more important than your job title.

When you have your own business, you are far more than your job title of CEO, COO, CFO, Creator or Founder - you are the HR, the Sales Person, the Creative Head, the Marketing Guy, the Help, the Tech Support, you basically become everything.

You not only have all the respectable job titles but also any or all menial jobs as well, when you are starting off.

You are everything and do everything and you find out that it is not easy being in business. It is harder than you initially thought.

But that's not all.

In addition to being in business and playing all the roles, you also have the personal life roles to play. You are also a daughter, a son, a husband, a friend, a wife, a neighbor, a partner, a mother, a father, and sometimes you feel overwhelmed with all that is expected of you. It is during these times that throwing in the towel crosses your mind.

This book helps you streamline these responsibilities and shows how you can successfully manage them. It helps you alleviate that feeling of doing so much but getting little or no productivity. It helps you from the inside out, making you truly productive and happy.

I Work For Me reminds you that you chose this path because you want to do what you love without being restrained by the societal box and parameters. While treading this path may come naturally for others, some of us struggle and learn our way to success.

Inspired by my own experience and growth, I Work For Me is for you if you have a business, or are thinking of starting your own business, or are working for yourself. I will share what I did when I started working for me and how I overcame the feelings and thoughts which initially blocked me from success.

I write to you, sharing steps and decisions I took, learning how to effectively run a business, even without the conventional education or a family background of business owners.

This book will help you by showing you how to work on and for yourself, and then how to work better for those that you serve.

Using the I.M.B.R.A.N.D formulae, I Work for Me will show you how to effectively and productively mind your business.

CHAPTER ZERO

I am a woman of faith; I believe that faith transforms lives and my life is proof of it.

You may or may not be a believer of a Supreme Power, God or a Power greater than you. This is not a a book on religion and my intent is not to talk about religion, but the fact remains that your thoughts create your world. You may call it the law of attraction, the Universe or what have you - the bottom line is, it works.

Phrases such as , "the road to success is a lonely road' or 'be willing to walk alone', honestly don't appeal to me as I don't believe in them . I believe we are all here to live a life of purpose, and once you are on your path, you will succeed. Similarly, others are also here to live their life's purpose. Some will get on your train of life and alight at the right destination for them; you only have to be clear about what you want.

Business or work is an integral part of our lives. If you are a solopreneur, an entrepreneur, a business man or a professional, then you are doing so because you love your work. You know how much your dreams and your life purpose means to you; however, the moment you start on your own, you realize that it is not easy.

When you run a business all alone, you know you are playing multiple roles as we have talked about in the introduction. You are not just a business owner, you are everything; a receptionist, a sales head, a creative head, a CEO, a COO, a CFO, Human Resource, Marketing Head and many more roles. In the midst of this chaos, to keep yourself at the best frame of mind for your work, you have to find a way to center yourself.

And to stay centered, I believe that God, Supreme Power, or a Power greater than you has to be the center of your business and any relationship.

This is something that I learnt from May McCarthy. In her book, *Path to Wealth*, she speaks about a Chief Spiritual Officer who is none other than God or the Supreme Power who is your partner in your work or in every work that you are doing. That being the case, then , 'the road to success is lonely," is false because you have the biggest force working with you.

Having a personal ritual will also help you stay centered.

I have named this chapter, Chapter Zero because everything in this chapter is the base that is required for you to be a successful business person enjoying a life of fulfillment. Please note that these are tips and my experiences. If you don't know where to start from, you can follow the step axis and, with practice, discover what works for you and what speaks to you. You are free to change and add to your everyday rituals. This proven method has worked for me and I am passing it on to you.

Having a morning ritual gives you a better disciplined life. Being disciplined matters and I will surely talk touch on this in one of the ensuing chapters because it is a vast topic and we will get to that later. This, however, is an initial start for you.

The three ingredients which need to be a part of your morning ritual are;

- Positive Thoughts
- Gratitude
- Faith

Positive Thoughts.

Throughout this book, you will see me mentioning this repeatedly; your thoughts create your world. The simplest narration to buttress this point is something you might have experienced. Have you ever thought of buying a new car, maybe a Range Rover, which is my personal favorite? You will notice that from the moment the thought crosses your mind you will start noticing and seeing Range Rovers everywhere. Each time a car passes by, or when you are driving you'll notice the Range Rovers. If you have ever experienced this, then you'll agree with me that your thoughts create your world.

Proverbs 17:22 says, 'A cheerful heart is a good medicine, but a crushed spirit dries up the bones.' Similarly, 'the soothing tongue is a tree of life, but a perverse tongue crushes the spirit,' says Proverbs 15:4.

Positive thoughts are that important.

When I say positive thoughts, I am talking about you thinking positively about your own business. Things will go wrong, I mean they are supposed to go wrong, challenges are supposed to arise, that's what makes life breathable. In the midst of these challenges, stay positive and keep calm... as everyone says, 'keep calm and think it through'. Having a positive attitude gives you the strength to do that.

Gratitude. One of the most beautiful ways of maintaining a positive attitude is through the practice of gratitude. This practice helps inculcate a positive attitude in our lives. Melody Beattie says, 'Gratitude unlocks the fullness of life. It turns what we have into enough and more, it turns denial into acceptance, chaos to order, confusion to clarity. It can turn a meal into a feast, a house into a home, a stranger into a friend. Gratitude makes sense of our past, brings peace for today, and creates a vision for tomorrow.' Which is what we want, right?

We want to have clear vision, as business people…. to see what we want to achieve. William Arthur Ward says, 'Gratitude can transform common days into thanksgiving, turn routine jobs into joy and change ordinary opportunities into blessings.' Gratitude is a powerful process for shifting your energy and bringing more of what you want into your life. Be grateful for what you already have and you will attract more good things.

Faith. As long as you do not wish harm on anyone, have faith that your dreams will come true. You will be successful, the Universe or even Earth is a sign of growth. You are born to grow. Anything and everything grow; trees grow, seeds grow. Children are born and they grow into humans, so all around you there are signs of growth.

Also, if you have any leftover in your kitchen, fungus starts to grow on it - that, again, is a sign of growth. It is a sign that what you feed grows. If you feed your positive thoughts, using gratitude as a tool, they will grow. If you feed your negative thoughts, that is what will grow; it will grow like the fungus which is not going to be useful for you.

Jeremiah 17:7, 8 says, 'Blessed are those who trust in the Lord and have made the Lord their hope and confidence; they are like trees planted at the river bank with roots that reach deep into water. Such trees are not bothered by heat or worried by long months of drought, their leaves stay green and they never stop producing fruit.'

I have picked these verses from the Bible, as this is what I know and believe in. I am sure that on the path you follow, you will come across similar verses in all revered books.

The intention is not to tell you what the religion or the Bible says, the intention is to make you aware that everything grows just as the trees that are not bothered by heat and long months of drought. Their leaves will stay green and they will never stop producing fruit. It is symbolic , it is metaphoric - if you are the one who doesn't get bothered with all the chaos around you, if you are the one who stays strong, even in the days when business is not working, when things are not flowing, when everything else is going wrong, you staying strong must and will pay off .

That is what faith is.

Even if you have faith as small as a mustard seed, you will see the results of it. I believe very strongly in this and will reiterate it as often as I am able to. It has worked for me innumerable times.

Now, how do I use these three ingredients in my daily ritual? This is what I do; I follow a simple step by step process, something inspired by the teachings of May McCarthy from her book, *Path to Wealth*, and Rhonda Byrne from '*The Magic.*'

So while the steps I take come from different genres, it works for me, and understanding the spirit in which I am imparting this is essential. Once understood, you too will discover what resonates with you and is for you.

Step One : This is generally at the start of the day. When I wake up, I start with the gratitude practice. I know it sounds odd since once up, there are a multitude of things to do. You probably feel that sitting down and writing the gratitude practice won't work, but, trust me, it does. You just need to find time for it. When I say you need to find time for it, I mean it literally.

It's your business, you are working for yourself. If you were going to get paid for it, wouldn't you do it? So, since you are going to get paid for it, you are just sowing the seeds at this time. So, do it.

Let's say you get up every day at 7 am, you can create time by getting up at 6 am. Why? Because you would be getting paid for it, it is as simple as that. So, get up at 6, finish your daily activities then your day always starts at 7 - so you are right on time.

Sit in a quiet place and have a gratitude practice. Write down things that you are absolutely grateful for. Make a list of them, the length of the list depends on you.

That's the first step.

Step Two : Here you write down how you think your day will unfold. Say that you are going to have an amazing day. Say that whatever you have set out to do for the day will work out for the best and the work will be completed for sure. Always use positive language when doing this practice.

Step Three is giving love. Take five minutes for this - you can time yourself if necessary, close your eyes, meditate and think of all the people that you know, all the people you are connected with, all those you are going to work with, imagine those you hope to work with in future, and give them love from your heart. Say it out that all these people should be blessed and loved. Wish them the best. Act like the Universe, providing them with all they need at that moment. Give love and light and bless each one in your heart.

It doesn't have to be just people you are happy with. It could be that family member you don't get along with or it could be the business partner you feel is creating challenges for you. You are not doing this in a negative way, you are blessing them and what you give is what you receive.

Step Four is to simply go ahead with the flow of the day. Have an amazing day. Things may turn out unexpectedly, the universe may have something different in store for you, don't worry about that, everything is going to be fine. Go on and have your day as your step four.

Step five happens at night. Before you go to sleep, while lying in bed, get your gratitude list, then go ahead and read it. You may not have it with you as you are already in bed and too lazy or tired to go get it, it is fine. Just close your eyes and in your mind, give thanks for everything that has happened during the day, both good and bad.

You stay thankful for all the good things because they will help you and they have made you happy. You stay thankful for the 'bad' things because they have given you lessons which you needed to learn to reach your potential. Give thanks.

Step six - pray.

When I say pray, I am aware that some of you might be uncomfortable with this. In such an instance, look forward to the next day and set your intentions for the next day, although praying helps. When I pray, all I do is ask for a peaceful sleep , being thankful for a beautiful day and having life for another day, and praying for the security of each and every person that I gave love to in the morning, and for each and every person who is in my life.

Step seven. When setting your intentions right, trust that everything would work out fine and go to sleep.

These seven steps have helped me and I have every trust that these will also help you. In due time, you will find your own way of doing things, which is absolutely fine. I don't expect you to follow what I am saying. All I expect you to do is find your own morning ritual.

Each and every successful person has a morning ritual, get yours. Don't let your phone be a distraction. We are in a digital world and most times when we wake up the first thing we do is to check our phones. We check Facebook or Twitter to see how many new followers we have or to see how the post we made last night is doing, to see how many people have replied to it, liked it or commented to it. We want to know what the world is doing.

Don't focus on the entire world, which is what we do when we are on social media. Trust me I am a fan of social media as you will realize when you read on. Social media helped me survive in a country where nobody knew me. I moved countries right at the peak of my career and I had to start from scratch in a place where I didn't know anyone - no family, no friend, no familiar face.

So, I am not against social media. What I am saying is that for you to be centered, you have to be the most important person in your life. By following this ritual, all you are doing is giving yourself some space because all these activities need about fifteen to twenty minutes in the morning, and another five at night. So thirty minutes in a day is not too demanding to set aside for yourself. Have a morning ritual; create your own if necessary.

In the subsequent chapters, we will know what we are supposed to do and how to do them.

Let's get the basics first, then let's get started!

"I"

IDEAS TO PLANNING

This chapter is divided into two parts.

Part 1

Everything starts with a small idea. Everything.

We all have our dreams, desires and goals which began as little ideas and these keep us going on with life every second of every day. We have many dreams and goals, yet as life keeps moving, new goals keep getting added to our list, so clarity will help us create a better path to drive through the road of life with the right stops at the right time.

In order to plan your business better and be successful at the same time, it's essential to have clarity and vision. Working alone and being responsible for the body and soul of your business can be overwhelming at times; small failures and challenges may make us rethink our work and the chances are high that these thoughts can lead us into a spiraling low or into quitting.

Here is where the power of hope kicks in. I am talking about how having a vision for yourself gives hope which acts as a ray of light, giving you something to look forward to. I mean, you cannot be in business and say, 'I don't know how or what I want tomorrow to look like.' Unlike other areas in your life where you can be vague, when it comes to business and how it works, that's not going to cut it. If you 'succumb' to the lack of clarity and vision (in other words, giving in to DOUBT), you will end up having the business running you, instead of the other way around. So on those days when business and work is down and discouraging, it is this ray of hope that keeps you going, it is with these ideas that you plan your next move.

Many among you would have undoubtedly read books, or even taken courses on how to set your vision, so I'm going to get straight to the point. I have a set of important questions which serve to make your vision clearer, and which help make it easier for you to plan your business.

These questions helped me gain clarity on my vision and mission, so I hope they will bring you the same. The best thing about these questions is that you can keep coming back to them every six months or as often as you need to, and trust me every time you answer them, you gain better clarity.

I know at this point you might be thinking, 'I know what I want!' Well, if you do then that's great, and truly amazing, so this will only help you move a step ahead. I firmly believe that answering the following questions will spark some new ideas in you and also help create your vision and mission statements in a clearer way.

To be most effective in this exercise, use a timer and give yourself ninety seconds to answer each question. Do not overthink them, just let the answers flow.

These are the questions;

- How do I want my life experiences to be if money and time are not a challenge?
- What does growth in life really mean to me?
- How can I contribute to the world?

- Who am I, and why am I here?
- What is my legacy?
- If I achieve my life goals, then how would I feel?
- How can I feel the feeling along the way right now?
- What keeps me going?
- What is it that I value the most?

Collate your answers to the above questions and put them together to create your vision and mission statements. Your responses will lead you to more questions. So ask yourself, what ideas do I have? Write it down. What is my vision? Write it down. What is my mission? Write it down.

Part 2

In this part, I talk about *I Work for Me.*

This is the part where you get to plan your business in greater detail. I am sure you have your business plan already, so let's look into it in a more detailed manner.

When I started my business, I worked hard, trying every possible option to grow my business and took every part that I felt had opportunity. Today, looking at that road I took, from a top view, I realize how haphazard my moves were. My steps were in every possible direction, and so, at times, I went in circles.

Business planning is just the first step in the whole process, and the real work starts after that. For most entrepreneurs, this may look like a common and basic step, but you will be surprised to know that many entrepreneurs start their businesses without planning, and I speak from personal experience.

I did not have a business plan for seven years, even after being in business that long. While it could be attributed to a lack of knowledge, I learnt fast through hard knocks. I've also met, in my journey as a business coach, too many entrepreneurs who have been in business about five to six years without a business plan. So I feel there is a need to talk about this.

Now, planning a business is ideally one of the most important tasks and it helps you make decisions concerning the business easily and quickly. Thankfully, there are many options available online today, on planning a business, and some software that can help - but I am giving you a head start here. However, as I said earlier, there is more to a business than a business plan despite its importance.

Let me explain.

I was not blessed with a business - oriented family; I am the first one in my family to start a business. I had zero know –how on running a business; I had no one to advise me or give me some direction; and Oh, yes! when I started off, I had no bank balance, so I started from scratch. What this meant was that for many years I only managed from hand to mouth.

Business skills did not come to me naturally - I had to learn every aspect of it. I was always a customer service person, sales was not my forte; it was not a natural skill. I also struggled with finances. I knew that I was very talented and better at my work than many of my competitors, but what I could not figure out was why I was not getting business as much as they did.

I'm not condoning comparing yourself to others but healthy competition spurs you to doing better and this did that.

Instinctively, I knew something was missing and I was not doing something right. It was strikingly obvious that hard work alone was not going to help, so I began retrospection.

I'd have a plan for the day and to-do lists for everything, but somehow I still fell prey to all the defaults; defaults like procrastination, self - doubt, lack of goals, thoughts of giving up, fear of failure, listening to doubters and naysayers, and the worst was a lack of self-control.

In my retrospection I asked myself what was missing.

I had been successful in my work career and I had no doubt that I was talented. When I had a job, I climbed the ladder of success faster than I was doing in my business, so what was I doing wrong now? Then I realized I was not working for my business as much as I used to work for my job.

It was an eye-opener!

In my job, I was dedicated, I had discipline, I showed up for the meetings, I held myself accountable for my behavior and actions, and that was exactly what was missing. While I loved the feeling of being the boss of my life, I was a boss that was not helping enough. I realized that I was actually a brand myself, and I really needed to work for me

I sat down and created a business plan.

Drafting a business plan is relatively easy. I mean it is as simple as typing in 'business plan' in Google and finding out which one suits you. Each field or profession has a different business planning category. My intent is not to teach you how to draw a business plan. You can find all the necessary tools online for about $7 or even free.

So I went online, and created a business plan. Thereafter I sat down and wrote an offer letter to myself. The letter appointed me as the business owner and founder. In it was all the responsibilities and goals which needed to be achieved, and it worked.

I now had goals to work towards and I wrote down how much I would be earning as my salary. It worked like a miracle for me, which is why I am sharing it with you... because I know it will work for you too.

It is time for you to create a job profile for yourself. In appointing yourself, you need to think like an entrepreneur and jot down every minute detail that you would demand if you were actually hiring an employee (well you are!).

Your job profile should be apt. Once again, you can go ahead and visit Google to find out how to create a job profile. Mine is attached in the pictures and you can take a look at it.

There are a few things which your job profile should include.

- **Your Role**: What do you appoint yourself as? CEO, COO, Chief Creator, HR, it is up to you.

- **Job Responsibilities**: Get into the minute details of the job responsibilities. Don't forget to include things like how you get to take care of yourself. Maybe you get only eleven days of holiday, or twenty-two. Maybe you are one who likes more holidays, fine! But ensure you are working. Include every minute detail.

I actually included even my Twitter and Facebook followers in the list. I was very clear that I did not want to use external tools to get followership. I needed my followership to comprise genuine and organic followers. I decided to take it slow but it worked for me.

I started with about fifteen followers on Facebook and none on Twitter. Today, two years later, I have crossed 5,000 and I'm in the process of getting more followers every now and then. So, yes, include every minute detail; write down every job responsibility, how many meetings to host, write down if you need to join certain groups, write down if you need to show up for your meetings, etc.

Write down every job responsibility.

- **Write Down the Salary**: Write down the amount that you have to earn every month, which will serve as your sales target. That is your salary.

This worked for me and I look forward to it working for you. Take some time, it may take a day or two, but make sure you do it. It took me somewhere around four hours to actually sit down and create a job profile for myself, thinking of and including every minute detail of what

I needed to work on. I have put some pictures of it, but only for your reference.

You and your business are unique, so create and draw your own, letting your enlightenment guide you on what you need to do for yourself. Mine is just a guide.

So, go get started.

"M"
MEASURE YOUR DAY

We have spoken about having a business plan, how to create it, and how to write an appointment letter to yourself. Now let's talk about how to really work for yourself, and why it is very important that you measure and maximize your day, each day, by chalking down your working hours.

One of the biggest challenges that I have seen with most people who move away from a complete working environment, especially if they had worked for someone else for years, is that the moment they start working for themselves they somehow get into a huge comfort zone. It is understandable - they don't report to anyone else and they don't have any external pressure.

So suddenly you leave your job and you no longer have a boss, or anyone to report to or reporting to you, and it fully dawns on you that you are the boss of your own time. Somehow you will be tempted to slip into a comfort zone.

To manage such temptations, it is important that you are aware of and understand the significance of how to manage time by measuring your day.

This is not about getting up early in the morning or starting your day at four-thirty a.m. One thing for sure though, is that each one of us, whether we are night owls or early birds, will have to work a certain number of hours to make sure the work is done. I know sometimes it does seem as though there are people who don't appear to work, and yet the job gets done. Well, that stage of our life awaits us if we get successful in life, and that is one reason we need to work hard today.

There are some great quotes on time which shows the need for its management.

Jim Rohn says, "Either you run the day or the day runs you."

"When it comes to time, there is good and bad news, the bad news is that time flies and the good news is that you are the pilot," says Michael Altshuler, and I love it!

I have always realized and resonated with what Zig Ziglar says, "People often complain about lack of time, when lack of direction is the real problem." How true!

You are never short of time; it is usually a lack of direction or a lack of understanding of what your priorities are. We know that there is a night routine and a day routine, so what is needed now is that we talk about getting things done in measured time.

From the previous chapter, you have now created your business plan, and have appointed yourself to work for your own company and are in the process of creating your own brand. This process needs for you to think about exactly what you wrote in your appointment letter, so you are reminded of what your responsibilities are, and you are reminded that you are paying yourself a salary, a salary that you are expected to earn off the job.

Now put on your thinking cap, if you are to hire someone else to do exactly what is written there in that job profile you drafted and you were going to pay them like you plan to for yourself, how many hours do you think you would expect them to work? Even more important than the hours is, how efficiently would you want them to work?

When I talk about measuring your day and chalking down your working hours, I'm actually talking about you jotting it down even if you just do part-time at your business. This is basically about a need for complete dedication, understanding and clarity. It is about your routine even if you think you need to work only two hours a day or five hours a week. Whatever you decide is fine, my point is that you have to get a plan for yourself, a plan to get the job done.

So, plan your day, plan everything, I mean literally everything. I will be attaching a picture at the end of this chapter which shows how you can give a breakdown of your day by detailing each hour in planning.

There are a few tips you should know about chalking down your hours;

- Write down your wake-up time
- Write down your sleeping time
- Write down every break that you plan to take
- Fix some meetings with yourself. You can do whatever you want to do with that time. You can decide to just breathe or you can read a book. It is totally up to you - just be sure to jot down even the time you set aside for yourself.
- If you have to cook and do your daily chores, write them down also. By including them into your plan, you will feel so much better and will also realize how much extra time you have.

So plan every detail of your day, measuring and chalking down your working hours.

I decided to work for myself for a minimum of eight hours daily. In my profession, some things which others would see as less important are actually job requirements for me. Checking social media, for instance, is on my to-do list since I want to get my numbers up.

Another is reading.

Being a writer and a speaker, reading is an important part of my job profile since I have to keep abreast of the world. Knowing the importance of these activities, I include them in my plans.

Interestingly too, I decided not to work more than nine hours for myself. The rest of the time is made into me-time or family time, whatever I deem fit. That's my choice, and you get to make yours.

When chalking down hours, be sure to consider every possibility. Consider your going-out time and your travelling time, and even if you work from home still consider the travelling for the meetings you will need to do in the future. That's the extent to which you need to go to and what I mean by managing your time by measuring your day.

Here are four points that elaborates on the tips given:

- Get a routine
- Break your working hours into manageable chunks
- Make appointments with yourself
- Schedule a down time, i.e. time you need to take your breaks. It is absolutely important to do this.

This is one way to get organized.

The second way of getting organized is by making sure that the process of chalking down your hours is an easy process.

Invest in a journal

Again, the internet comes to our rescue. There are many available journals online; check them out and get the right one.

Get a journal.

Imagine getting five different notepads, one talking about your office work, another about your dreams, desires or goals, another about ideas, let's imagine that each notepad costs you about $5 - you will be spending close to $50 already.

Instead, take out about $40 and get an amazing journal and invest in it. Your journal should have everything under one roof; your ideas, your dreams, your desires, your goals, your vision and mission statements, your mood trackers, your positive habit trackers, your monthly reviews, your weekly plans, your important appointments, everything!

There are journals which can get that done. For the past three years I have been using one journal for lessons and mastery and believe me when I say it has helped me organize my time so much better. Go ahead and find a journal for yourself, and then take the time to write things down.

Looking at the challenges I have faced with a lot of people that I have worked with, especially with my clients, trust me, the longest time is spent when I work on getting them organized, getting them to sit down and write down their dreams, desires and goals to make sure that everything is in one place. They really find that tasking.

So I will be honest - writing down everything; writing down your vision and mission statements; planning your day; all this is time consuming but it is productive. Think about it. Investing two to three hours in a year, to sit down and think about how you want your following year to be can't be that daunting. .

If you're not ready to invest in yourself, I have a simple question for you: If you are building a brand for yourself and you are not ready to invest in it, how do you expect the world to invest in you?

I probably sound curt or am bordering on rudeness right now, but you need to see things for just the way they are. You have to start investing in yourself. So, once again, get yourself a daily journal, and write these things down, write everything down.

I am aware that you may not be in the habit of journaling, and that is okay. There will be times when you won't touch or write in the journal for days or a week, missing out some entries. It has happened to me too! But eventually I learned to control myself, making sure that I began enjoying the process because it helped me stay focused.

You may ask how the business plan we created, the chalking down of hours or even the morning routine we talked about gets to really help you. You may be convinced that you do not need to do all of these, and I understand. I understand because I have read many books on how to get your life organized or how to get your manifesto working for you or how to be grateful etc. I used to think, "Hey! I say thank you every time, and I am grateful for everything!" But I didn't have a routine for it, and having a routine has changed me.

Let me tell you how.

It started with small things, I will not get into my conscious and subconscious findings as this is not the place for that conversation, but everything you do comes back to the basics of you having clarity about your life.

You may say that you know exactly what your dream is, and I totally know that feeling. But doing this on a regular basis; daily, weekly, or even monthly, will evoke a change in you. It will change the way you react or respond to the world. It will affect your view of opportunities, and you realize that while you may miss out on a few opportunities, you will be capturing as many as possible.

You will also be able to enjoy your life, having reduced the stress. Your confidence level will soar, and when relating with people, you do not end up over committing or over promising, because you will be subconsciously aware of your measured time and what you chalked down, and this will guide you at the right moments.

I don't know if this has happened to you, but it has to me; you are focused, you have your dreams and are on your way to conquer the world, but when relating to people, you aren't able to find the right words at the right time, or you may not even remember what to say or worse, you end up over committing. Maybe you'd say to someone, "I will meet you next Saturday," but ten or fifteen minutes later, you realize that there is already a commitment to someone else at that time. You end up giving apologies, trying to reschedule and all.

Sometimes you realize you really don't want to do what you said you would. At this point, realization and clarity are working too, but it is too late. This makes you feel less confident and if you do it often enough, you'd get drained. Every time you apologize to someone, your energy levels fall and you feel a little less confident or capable.

So from my experience, these things help build your confidence, helping you make the right choices at the right time. This, in a way, trains your brain to give the right information at the right time and place. This is exactly what people say about success, it is about being at the right place at the right time.

This is about training our brain, body and mind to be there, and pick on opportunities which help us live the life of purpose we long for.

In summary, measuring our day by chalking down the hours is about two things:

- Actually, writing down those numbers of hours. You can use the attached diagram for reference. You can use the ideas or create your own.
- Use a journal, just one. Put everything in one place. That is how we ensure that we have control over our time.

This is still the planning mode and soon enough we will get to the action points, but this is the foundation – the start.

Measure your day. Chalk down those hours.

Measure Your Day

6:00 am	Wake Up
6:00 am - 8:00 am	Cook Breakfast, Walk, Brush
8:00 am - 9:00 am	Breakfast and Kitchen Clean
9:00 am - 10:00 am	Shower and Reading
10:00 am - 11:00 am	Exercise
11:00 am - 01:00 pm	Emails and Calls
01:00 pm - 02:00 pm	Lunch
02:00 pm - 05:00 pm	Work, Sessions and Calls
05:00 pm - 06:00 pm	Meditate and Breathe
06:00 pm - 07:00 pm	Cook Dinner
07:00 pm - 08:00 pm	Write or Read
08:00 pm - 09:00 pm	Dinner
09:00 pm - 11:00 pm	Write and Gratitude
11:00 pm	Sleep

"B"

BUILD AWARENESS

BE YOUR BRAND

When I say 'build awareness', I am talking about you actively being a brand ambassador for yourself. As I work for me, I have to show up for myself. I have to be there in the market. I can't expect social media to bring all of my businesses to me. I have to create my presence. I have to be physically present because word of mouth spreads faster, people buy people first and so I have to be out there to sell myself.

To build awareness, you have to start showing up by making those social appearances. If you have scheduled an event, go for that event; if you've got a free ticket, go for that event; if you like an event on Facebook or LinkedIn or something a friend had passed on, go ahead and attend it.

One of the things I have noticed about people who work for themselves is that they never feel they are ready or have the right attire and that is why most times they cancel appointments. They don't feel motivated because they are so comfortable doing what they do in their own space that they don't want to get out of their comfort zone.

So, here's what I did.

Although I work from home, 20% is me being physically anywhere else, especially for speaking arrangements, while the remaining 80% is done from home. I realized early that I wasn't not doing justice to my own job. If I were working for someone else and had to go to work, I would have gotten up at five in the morning, done everything required at home, gotten ready, perfectly ready, dressed up beautifully and gone to work. Even if it were not an event, I would make sure that I was doing everything well, and that is what is missing when you work for yourself.

You wear what you wear, you do what you do, you don't feel like changing, every day feels like another Saturday or Sunday, and sometimes when people come around, you make excuses for being dressed the way you are.

Let's not do that.

Let's get up every day and dress ourselves as if we are going to show up, as if we are going to work because that is what is happening. You are working for yourself, which means you are a brand and 'dressing up' is a baby step. You look in the mirror every day, you look at what you have and then you get dressed. In situations like these you will never wonder 'what do I need to wear', 'how do I look' or ask yourself 'should I really go?'

Why is it important to build awareness by making social appearances? It is because they lead you to the rewards of being your own brand. Social appearances give you that motivation that has driven you to do your business. Naturally, you will meet critics and you will also meet people who are pleased by your work. Do remember that for every time you please someone, there is one who is not. You are not there to please people; you are there to please your brand.

Speak about your brand, let people know about it. Let them come to you asking, 'Hey I think I know you, I've seen you on Facebook' or 'Hey, I think I know you, you spoke in the last event here'. You don't have to be a writer to speak somewhere, you don't have to be a model to look beautiful and show up somewhere. Just do it.

This is part of your investment in your brand. This is part of being your brand.

The last part I need to talk about when it comes to being your brand is you rewarding yourself. Every time you follow through with your plan, at least when it comes to your business, remember to reward yourself, because that will make and keep you more grateful towards everything that you have, and it will also make you aware of what you are receiving.

Many times we get caught up with the numbers and the stats that we have set for ourselves, that we don't measure our achievements as positive. If, for instance, you make a plan to get five people next month as new clients and you get four new people and a prospective client, you may keep complaining about how you got four but none of them has paid yet , which means that you got nothing this month.

What you are actually doing in moments like these is that you are not acknowledging your own success. Remember that whatever you focus on expands. If you keep focusing on things which didn't work, eventually things which didn't work will keep growing.

One reason why most businesses do not succeed or cross the five or seven-year mark is that they are so caught up in catching only wrong things - they are so caught up in criticizing themselves. Start rewarding yourself. You can use really small rewards, maybe financial rewards or pleasure rewards.

Financial rewards are things like, 'if I make five new clients this week, I will make sure that I buy myself a new headset' or 'if I get what I need or accomplish my goal for this month, I'll go to the spa.'

I don't know what kind of person you are, but go ahead and invest in yourself, take time for pleasure, make sure you go for that one vacation. Vacations are also social appearances. Go for it, be out there in the world.

Pleasure rewards are things like I'll spend more time with my family, or I will attend the Super Bowl this time – whatever that gives you pleasure, things like this, do it. Show up, make the social appearances and build your brand, then reap the rewards for being your brand. Enjoy your rewards on your journey.

Don't wait for ten years down the line, saying, 'when I am successful, then I will go...' Don't do that.

Enjoy now because everything is in the now. If you are taking the action steps now, then you should also have the pleasure times now.

That is what building appearances and being your brand is about, it is about showing up now, putting in the work now, and getting the rewards now.

"R"

RULES OF LIFE

The thought of rules of life may bring thoughts of rigid, stringent, boring and maybe disagreeable measures to be taken for success. You may also be thinking about the fact that you are not famous, and how you don't want to be someone with lots of rules for life to be adhered to. You have probably seen a lot of YouTube videos in that category too, like Steve Jobs' rules of life or, for the Indians, you may know Tata Ambani's rules of life, Sachin Tendulkar's rules of life, Priyanka Chopra's rule of life, Oprah Winfrey's rules of life and the list goes on. .

But here's the thing, it is not about being famous or not. You might just want to be successful enough to have good money and you are not interested in fame, but rules of life are not just for celebrities or famous people you may not want to be like. Rules of life is nothing but you being aware of yourself and creating rules for your own life.

In the last seven to eight years I have started moving into the path of spirituality and an understanding of what my life purpose is and learning how to go about it. At my initial stage I used to go crazy when I observed some people I respected and wondered, "How does he/she do that?" or I would, at times wish "I want to be like him / her!"

I also remember spending days and months or even years listening to YouTube videos, which sometimes served as my morning motivation. I would listen to somebody else saying, "These are my rules of life and this is what has made me who I am." Believe me when I say that they have helped me. They have helped me find direction, they have helped me decide what it is that I want from my life though it took its own time, and that's exactly why I'm writing this book.

Most times we tend to look for those we consider gurus, to tell us what is required or we look for that guide or mentor who'd say, "Just do this or that." We want someone who will help us find answers. In times when we don't have a direct approach or interaction, all these videos and books help us in building who we are.

Now, there's a secret you should know, you can go ahead and follow all the rules of somebody else's life, I mean those rules of life we mentioned above, those set by others, but the fact is that your life is your life and no one knows it better than you. So you've got to sit down and create your own rules of life.

There are two persons whom I love and am inspired by. I admire them in many aspects and there are a few rules they have set for themselves. The first person that I really love, admire and maybe idolize is Oprah Winfrey. I doubt you're surprised by this, so let's get to the point.

Oprah says that to be successful there are ten rules you need to follow:

1. Understand the next right move
2. Seize your opportunity
3. Accept that everyone makes mistakes
4. Work on yourself
5. Run the race as hard as you can
6. Believe
7. Realize that we are all seeking the same thing

8. Find your purpose
9. Stay grounded
10. Relax, it's going to be okay

So that's something that Oprah says has helped her be successful.

Similarly the second person that I really love is Priyanka Chopra. Priyanka is mainly an actress, but she's also an author. Once again, getting to the point, she says she has twelve rules which have made her who she is.

1. There is only one you. It is about who you really are; your core self, your core values, your beliefs, your flaws that make you stand apart.
2. Let your dreams fly. Don't confine your dreams in a shell. The universe is guiding you every day with opportunities knocking at your door, but you have to understand the signs to grab them.
3. Be ambitious. There is absolutely nothing wrong with being ambitious.
4. Be greedy. Be hungry for ambitions; you can have it all when you want it all. As long as your greed is not harming anyone, it's completely okay to want everything.
5. Do not compromise your dreams. Fight for your dreams; don't live to achieve somebody else's benchmark. Who can tell you who you should be? It is as simple as that.
6. Fail, fail, fail and rise like a phoenix. As certain as day and night is the fact that you will fail and that doesn't matter, rather what matters is your reaction to the failure. Push the failure aside, get up and move on. Don't ever avoid failure, instead analyze it.
7. Be bold and take risks. You will have to take calculated risks to evolve. Priyanka says she backs all her risk with 100% effort and dedication.
8. Surround yourself with the right people. Surround yourself with people who will motivate you, people who will help you progress and will not stab you in the back.

9. You cannot please everyone. I particularly love this one. With things like social media it's easy to be confused with people's opinion. Faces hiding behind anonymity and passing comments do not matter. Always remember that no matter what you do someone will always be unhappy.

10. Don't take yourself too seriously. Appreciate the funny thing called life, there will be good times and there will be bad times. So enjoy the rollercoaster, learn to laugh at yourself and learn to have fun.

11. Give back. Quoting what Priyanka said, "My mother always told me that there will always be someone who will be less fortunate than you, so give back in any way to the society and spread compassion and humanity."

12. Don't forget your roots and where you came from. I totally agree with this rule.

These are rules by Oprah Winfrey and Priyanka Chopra, who live different lives and have different rules. The point and fact is that you know your life and only you can create rules for your own life.

I totally love what Priyanka says - she keeps talking about taking everyone and getting the support that you require. She must have had her fair share of challenges, but she clearly had her family's support - that is something I did not have. So you get to define your own life and create your own rules based on your unique existence.

I have my own rules of life which are all mine and I'm going to share them, but I do want you to understand that after this I want you to sit down, take a look back at your life, and see what it is that you have always lived by and revisit it. This is the moment for you to understand and reevaluate your belief system. Check which beliefs help you grow and drop off the beliefs that once helped you but are not helpful anymore.

It is sometimes good to say, "This is how I have always been." As long as that way is helping you grow, multiply, prosper and be abundant, it is good; but if it's not helping you do that, then it's time to bring in that change. Creating rules for life helps define who we are and helps us discover the boundaries we want to set up or cross.

There is this belief that being in business and being a part of the business world, you need to play by the rules, but the million dollar question is, 'Whose rules are we talking about?'

Honestly, I have learnt from experience that it is best to play by your own rules and if you don't have these rules you will go crazy trying to keep up with people, fighting for yourself, and end up creating boundaries eventually. So right now, take a moment and make your rules.

Do realize also that you don't have to go for ten or twelve rules at a time, you can go with what you have right now and what life has taught you. The school of life is the best database you need to create rules for yourself.

I did that too and with time, as I learnt, I added some new rules and deleted some old ones which didn't serve me anymore. It is a required process you will go through as everything needs to be changed or refreshed every now and then. Your rules may change or remain the same in future, as long as they are relevant and something that you would want to stick by.

So, once again, take a moment and create your own rules.

There are five things you need to consider when creating your own rules;

- Your life experiences
- Your beliefs. Sit down and analyze what your beliefs are. Find out who you are at the core.
- Your values. What are the values that you want to live by, what is it that you want to be known for, what is your legacy?
- Your strengths. Understand what it is that makes you strong.

- Understanding your vision in life and the required tools to achieve it.

These five points should be considered before you sit down and make your rules for life. Understand that for each one of us, each dream is different, that's why you have to take a moment and think through for yourself.

I will now share my rules of life.

1. I am me. There is only one me. There is no one on earth who can be another Snehal Singh, and that is something I remind myself of every day.

2. My birth does not define me. Where I was born does not define me. My work and what I do with my life today is what defines me. So, I get to live the life of my dream, and I strive each day to make sure my dreams come through.

3. I can have it all. This is something I am in total agreement with Priyanka and Oprah. I believe that everything is achievable. Whether you trust me or not, this is a fact. As long as I don't hurt anyone on the way and I give love and care and a lot of healing to the world, I'm doing good and I can have it all. I can have an amazing family who will love me and this rule has helped me change things over a period of time.

4. I love myself. This may sound a bit repetitive, but it is a rule. I'm not on this earth to please anyone else. I also know this probably sounds like an absolutely stupid rule, but it is a fact which matters to me. It may not matter to you, but where I come from, with the upbringing I had and with most of my challenges being because I put everybody else before me, I totally agree with those who say that you cannot give others what you don't have.

Taking care of yourself is the first step to taking care of the world. You cannot be half full to give others what you don't have enough of. So my job is not to please everyone, my job is to live my life of purpose and do what I am required to do, and once again it all comes down to not hurting anybody on this earth and doing good.

5. Failure is a step towards success. Failures have defined me, failures have told me what I need to do, and I have succeeded after having a lot of failures in my life. It is okay to fail or breakdown. I have had a lot of failures and I have been rejected a lot of times, even personally, and I don't mind sharing this with you.

There was a person that I wanted to marry, whom I knew for eleven years, and we struggled for approximately seven of those years to make sure that everyone accepted me. So for seven years I kept getting rejected. I know what failure is and I'm not saying that I have always been strong; no I haven't - I have been a cry baby and have complained about things too! One thing I have learned though, is that if you have a failure moment it is okay. It is okay to fall, it is okay to sit and cry and maybe use up the whole tissue box, or have a full bottle of wine or a tub of ice-cream or just sit and watch movies back to back with popcorn, or whine and not talk to anyone, it is all fine.

You have to live your failure too, and once you do that, dust yourself, stand up tall with your head held high and say to yourself, "It's time to move on." Don't forget your failure, learn from them. Leave the bitterness out of it and learn. It is absolutely fine to fail.

6. Tithe. Give back. Show gratitude. I totally believe in this. Even when I was not earning, I used to get clients who were non-paying ones, and after every five pro-bono clients, I made sure that I actively went asking for clients to serve for free. It's always good to give back. Earn as much as you want but go ahead and give back to the

society and the world. There are different ways to give back, just don't miss out on the opportunity to do so.

7. Honesty. One of my most important values is honesty. I cannot handle dishonesty and I am incapable of being dishonest to anyone. I may come across as curt or blunt at times, but I say things just the way they are. I am honest not only to the world but I'm also honest about me to myself and that is important. You have to learn to be honest with yourself.

8. Your thoughts create your world. I really love this rule of mine. I have learnt that if you change your language to yourself, you can change your world and that is why it is one of my rules. I changed my thoughts and I changed my world. Your thoughts will change your world, go ahead and try it.

9. Never forget your roots. I totally agree with Oprah Winfrey, Priyanka Chopra and many other successful people on this. I practiced this even before I got exposed to all those videos that I watched. Trust me, when you're doing something which is rule based and living a life by your own rules, there will be people who will punch you, laugh at you, poke you and say, "that is not how it works, she is crazy, she is stupid." Or they'd ask, "Who does that in today's world?" I have always been made fun of when I have chosen to stick to my roots of who I am and where I belong. It doesn't mean that you have to get stuck in a mentality or get caught up in things, but never forget where you came from. That's what keeps me grounded, it keeps me humble, it keeps me grateful and it makes sure that I give love every time I speak to anyone and that keeps me going. So never forget where you came from, this is very important.

So these are my rules.

So it's your turn to go ahead and create your own rules of life. Bear in mind that you won't be able to create it in an hour and if you are trying to do that then you must be really self-aware.

You have read the chapter, and it is time to start thinking, start noticing, start observing yourself over a period of time. Each day, while you are thinking or listening to someone else there might be a moment when it would click and you'd say, "Hey! That's a rule I want to live by." When such a situation arises, note it down, sit down and find out which other rules you want to live by. Once you have done that, make sure you put them in pointers everywhere that you can see them - when you get up and get ready, at your working desk etc.

It's okay if you have to explain to your family members. None of these rules is going to be negative so if somebody else is going to follow them, then that is going to work out well for them too! So enjoy the life of rules.

I have heard a lot of times, that rules are not meant to be followed but to be broken, but trust me if you really want to enjoy your life to the fullest and still be grateful, you have to live by the rules. Not by the rules of the world or the rules of the society but your own rules. You have to have personal ethics you work by and these rules are not necessarily related to your business.

This chapter is totally about you being who you are at the core, not dividing yourself into professional and unprofessional aspects. This is who you are no matter who you are with; your best friend, the love of your life, your child, your mother, your father, your sister or anyone whom you love or even anyone whom you do not like at all, but if you are living by the rules you will find it difficult to hate anyone because you will be happy and content with who you are. You are creating our existence just as I am creating mine.

Go create your existence.

Go write down your rules of life.

"A"

ACCESSIBLE/
APPROACHABLE

The first step in your business is being committed to your own success and you will agree with me that commitment is a choice. In the same vein, when it comes to being available, it is your choice of which method to use or not to use, to be perceived as being accessible or approachable.

You can choose to be either online or offline. Either go 'techy' or not.

When talking about tech, I am talking about the world today. I am talking about the fact that you don't need to leave your house to do your business. I am living proof of that fact. As mentioned in a previous chapter, I moved to a different country. I never saw myself leaving my birth country and leaving behind the business prospects I saw there; but I moved with my husband to a new country and I made progress... great progress.

Also, as you know, my educational background was not exceptional except for some certifications I had earned over a period of time. I knew I didn't want to work for anyone anymore. I had done that for about twelve to thirteen years, and I now just wanted to work on my own. Funnily, I didn't think I would be moving when I made the decision to work for me. One of the things which helped me succeed in a land where I literally knew no one, other than my husband, was social media. Social media was how I was able to get access to clients and how clients could access me.

Starting from scratch is highly tasking and social media did help me immensely. It helped me get out there, meet people, connect and form networks all from scratch. My connection started on a personal note; I joined groups and left some, joined book clubs and hung out, related with people to see if I liked them. I did a lot of exploring made possible because of social media. It happened because I had a website, it happened because I used the basic tech stuff to be approachable, and that is the angle I am sharing .

My path is definitely not the only way to work. You could be someone who is not really into social media. It could be that you are not interested in clicking those pictures on Facebook or Instagram, and that's fine too. As I said it boils down to choice.

Basically, what is best for business, is that we are always seen as being approachable. We want people to know that we have something, a product or a service, whatever it is you have to offer, that we believe would help them and you should discover the best way to get this truth across to them. You may choose to step out and create your own or join social groups where you are physically present and get a networking, or you can do this virtually by using the latest available technology. In fact, I did both, so I can give you tips on the two options. I started off with technology, and then I started stepping out. I had my reasons which included trying to get a better understanding of the land I recently moved to.

Although I am about to share how social media helped me, I should let you know that I wasn't always that involved in social media.

Seven years ago, I was not a social media enthusiast. I had a Facebook account which I never used, I never posted anything on it. I didn't know what Twitter was and I didn't care. I didn't have a website but I had a blog where I posted write-ups because people encouraged me to. Even at that I'd post just a tiny fraction of what I wrote because I was too lazy to go there. Social media was not a necessity because I was in my home country and I was socially active with friends. I knew people, I had connections and I had built my network but all these changed when I moved and my profession changed. I had to start from scratch.

My point is, both styles of social networking are required and yes, you can do one without the other. It is all about your choice. Hopefully, you have read the previous chapters of this book and you know what you want, you know your goals and know when you want to reach the milestones to get there.

At this point, you should know what you want years down the line and use this clarity to decide which way you want to go; use this knowledge of yourself to make a decision whether to go online or do it offline. Do you want to physically meet people? All the answers are completely dependent on what your goal is.

So if you don't have this clarity yet, pause, put a bookmark on this page and write down your goals. Write down what you want in the coming months or in the coming years. I started out with ten and twenty years down the line and that is where my journal came into play, helping me write it all down. I have also, in a previous chapter, talked about journals and how they make things easier.

If you have help available to attain this level of clarity, use them. You don't have to do it all on your own. If you are the creative kind, go for it. Ensure you get to that point where you have a clear view of where you want to go.

Now let's talk about going online.

When I talk about going online, I am talking about the basic factors, such as having your own website. Is it necessary? I'll get into that in detail. We could also talk about all your social media platforms like Facebook, Instagram, Twitter, LinkedIn, etc. Interwoven in these discussions would be talks about connecting, associating and being available; reaching people and being visible on online spaces other than yours; visiting websites of others; and having your business cards with you, ready at all times.

It doesn't matter how much business you do, what service you offer or what part of the world you live in, you have to print. Printing is now cheaper and easier, thanks to technology, and since you are in business, printing these cards is a good investment to make. Trust me.

Let's take it one step at a time, and let's start with website creation.

There is the option of creating your website by yourself. If you are simply creating things like landing pages or just putting up some ad, you may be able to do it on your own but if you are thinking of a full-fledged, dynamic website, I recommend you hire someone. Don't try to be a jack of all trades and a master of none. You don't want to do that especially when it comes to your business which is your baby as you want to make sure it succeeds. Hire the professionals and get it done right. Even if you are hiring a professional, you should be mindful of the fact that while a website is a worthwhile investment, you shouldn't expect miracles.

Your website is your online profile; it is a place where people come to see you. At the start, most of the connections you get will come from people who already know you, and then they'd go visit your website, that's the first step. If you hired the right people and the Search Engine Optimization (SEO)expert has done the job right, you will start getting unknown enquiries. In Google search, your name will start popping up and it can transform to giving you businesses. So, yes, the website is an investment at the start.

However, you have to do your own analysis; find out how much you are willing to invest, bearing in mind also that it is a one off thing. When you create one, you don't have to worry about it for two to three years minimum, except if you change your business or service line.

Go ahead and invest in a website, make sure that it is mobile friendly too. In creating a website, you don't have to know it all. I cannot and will not tell you that all that is involved in creating a website is in this book, which is one of the reasons you should hire an expert. And if you want, you can reach out and connect with me and I will give you tips on which way to go and what goes for which kind of website, as I am good at that.

That is for step one.

Step two is your choice of social media. You may not enjoy being so social, putting up posts and whatnots, but I invite you to take a look at my personal Facebook page and my company page. You will find nothing personal there. As I keep reiterating, it is about choices you make; it is your account and you can keep it the way you want.

I don't post anything personal, yet Facebook is the biggest business portal for me right now. Most of my speaking gigs have come from Facebook. I have gotten most of my projects from Facebook and most of my client base has come from Facebook. Most of my clients are people on Facebook who check my profile and like how I speak and that's why they connect with me.

The same goes for Instagram. Instagram has given me some amazing windows when it comes to website designing, writing promotions and so on.

Social media is helpful and doesn't need a lot of investment since all these accounts are free. Take advantage and use them to project and promote your ability. I do understand if you are somewhat reluctant to share your pictures. By the same token, it does not mean you have to be an extrovert to use the social media. Post what you think and say what you feel, responsibly, as it doesn't matter what your profession is.

For instance, I have a friend who is a hairdresser, and she keeps sharing posts on what she thinks, like how life has helped her, her belief about things, how hard work is important etc. She keeps writing, not minding that she is not an amazing writer, she just keeps writing. She puts herself out there, and people are constantly reminded that she is there.

Some wonder if it matters what kind of business you are in, to be socially active? No, it doesn't. Do you have to put up anything personal? No, you don't. If people like you, they will patronize your business and buy your services. The whole point is the need for you to be there, accessible and approachable.

If you get recommended by someone, for instance, and they say, 'This person is amazing and is really good, why don't you use her services?' The first thing the person you are being recommended to will do is to get your name, go to social media, find your name and how you look, try to see how you think, and then decide if they want to call you or not. This happens for sixty to seventy per cent of the crowd.

There are about six million people online, so you have a waiting market where people can find you, and they can trust you. Many people feel they don't need a social media presence to excel, and if you don't think you need it, you can move on from this segment of the chapter onto the next, but if you ask me, I'll say a resounding 'yes', because that is where the business lies.

Five to ten years down the line, everything will be online. As a matter of fact, everything is already online today, and that is how tech-savvy the world is. At that time, remaining traditional won't make sense, but if you feel strongly about this, it is still your life and your business and it is your choice.

Now I think the question about SEO should be addressed before I move on to how to market offline. The question is, is it necessary to invest in SEO or put up some Google ads or Instagram ads or Twitter ads?

It is important you understand creating awareness. When I am talking about tech stuff, I am talking about creating your own brand. When I say 'I Work for Me', I am creating my own brand; I am my own employer and I am my own employee. I make sure that anyone who meets me and comes across me knows Snehal as a brand. That is what you should be doing; creating an awareness, creating a brand awareness.

So the decision to invest in SEO is solely your call.

I don't know what your business plans are, I don't know what your goal is, but I know that it is a simple calculation. Whatever your business plans are, one year down the line, if you don't invest even 0.5% of that in marketing, there is a high chance that you will be losing out on some good profit. So take calculated risks and try out new things.

For me, SEO was not used for a long while because I was getting good business from my social media and neither did I use Facebook Ads until quite recently. I only used it because I embarked on a project which needed a lot of publicity and marketing. Apart from this instance, I don't use Facebook Ads.

So, from my perspective, do you need the ads? Do you need the 'likes'? I'd say not really. If you ensure that there are regular activities on your page, people will be drawn to you, people will come to you, people will know you, and people will follow you. You do not need 10k or 20k followers for you to get businesses, although the numbers may matter eventually on some platforms like Twitter where the higher your number of followers, the more tendency you have of being listened to. So it is possible to get that many followers by taking small steps, but in the meantime do your thing, the right thing, and attract people to you.

Here's what you can do; make a social media calendar and assign a time to attend to it. You can say, for instance, 15 minutes every day or an hour each week, where you check your social media, update what needs to be updated, make one or two posts and that is about all that is required of you. The aim is simply to state your intentions, letting people know that you are available for them.

Organize yourself. Create your priority list. Find out what will bring you business and work with it. For me, it is LinkedIn, Facebook and Instagram but when it came to publishing, Twitter gave me a good amount of business. I did my research, finding out where which market lies, and I think you should also do that.

When it comes to social media know-how, there are YouTube videos, there are free online courses where you can learn something new and then apply it. Use these available resources to upgrade yourself, learn them, know them and use them.

Don't let age be a limiting factor. If there are things you don't know, you can ask the younger generation who is more knowledgeable in these, although some teenagers can be cranky. Take it as a sacrifice, build the relationship with them for the knowledge you need, go past their crankiness and take the help you need. If this approach doesn't work, then stick to the YouTube videos which are about 10 minutes long that show you how to use different social media.

One other thing you should be aware of is your need for patience when it comes to social media. In social media, everything takes time. People believe those who keep showing up, so you need to keep showing up to be taken seriously. Whatever platform it is that you learn is good for your business, being regular builds your credibility and that is good for business, no matter the number of followers or likes.

When people visit my social media page, they see things which they like. They send messages, telling me how they find it interesting but this feedback didn't happen overnight; it didn't happen during the early days when I posted every day. It took about three to four years for me to build that credibility, and all it needed was me taking out an hour a week, where I sat , checked other Facebook profiles, sent requests, interacted with them, made updates, and made posts. I just ensured that I was posting what I truly believed and I was not sending out a view of myself that was not real.

I am in the field of motivation and I am into training and teaching. I have a lot of clients as I am a business coach, and I help various kinds of business owners to build their business. That's what I do. So if I can help a jewelry designer, a marketer, a school owner, a company owner, a person into production, and a photographer, using the same methods, then I think you are safe. I've also helped a hairdresser, a fashion stylist, a dance academy owner, so if I can help all these people who come from different areas of life, then I can help you too.

I am teaching you the basics, the very basic things about tech which I have no doubt will help you. You don't have to be an expert to be effective. You don't have to find a 'Instagram for dummies' or 'fb for dummies' book - you don't need all those. You just need little help and everything is available online. Just set some dedicated time for research and do your research, but bear in mind that research never ends, so you have to be sure of what you are looking for, then end your research when you are done, after which you go back and implement.

Always show up. Always be accessible and approachable. I am aware that I am talking about a virtual world, but that also includes showing up. If you haven't posted anything on your page for two months, it means nobody is visiting your page and nobody knows you exist, and if nobody knows you exist, then you are definitely not getting business out of it, so show up. Once you start making businesses out of it, you can invest to show up even more, but first, you have to show up.

Also, interacting on others' platform is a way to get known. By interacting, you make friends who would check you out on your own platform. You stay in their minds and when a business opportunity comes, you also come to mind because somehow during your interactions, they know what you do.

See it as an investment, a seed you are planting and each post or comment is another small seed that you are planting. Everyone who reads it gets a little glimpse of who you are and how you think and they will decide if they want to do business with you.

Use your phone reminder or any other reminder, if you have to, to remind you to post. I do have reminders which remind me to post and when I don't have anything to post, I do a quick research and make a post. It takes only a few minutes to get it done. It is all about your dedication and as I said, commitment is a choice. Are you committed to making sure that when you work for yourself you are putting in 100%? That is a simple question.

Let's go to the second half of the topic; being social offline.

The way you have to show up in the virtual world is how you show up when you are offline too. If you don't like the new methods of social interaction, you have to go through the conventional methods. This means you have to get up and go for those meetings, you have to meet new people, and you have to let people know that you have products and services which you are ready to share because you are sure it will be helpful to them.

You may have to join some business groups and show up for their meetings. You may not like the crowd, but you have to realize that you are not just there to make friends but also to make money. Keep your goals straightforward. Once a week attend a meeting, join Chambers of Commerce, join the Business Networking Institute, and other similar associations. If you are a reader and someone into motivational business, join a book club. Show up and go there with your business cards, always be prepared. They could lead to your next business.

Whatever you do, make sure you show up. If you tell someone that you'll be there, make sure you get there as that is the credibility and trust you have to build, and if someone wants to give you business, they will have trust that you will be there. That is all there is to branding or social marketing - it is all about showing up, it is all about being visible. Remember out of sight is out of mind, be it on social media or otherwise. If you don't do the best you can for your business, don't expect people who come to you to do the best for you without knowing you.

So the manner in which you want to appear accessible and approachable is your choice, but make sure you are showing up and giving it 100%

"N"

NOW IS THE TIME

In the previous chapters, we discussed all the things that we had to do, from planning to measuring your day and coming up with your rules for your life. This chapter is about actually taking the action we need to take to turn our plans into action steps.

Planning is sometimes tasking for some people and they just like the action time. While planning is important, people who take action in everything they do are usually successful. This is why it is said that one may have great ideas, million dollar ideas, but if they are not followed through they won't get fulfilled. I am not about to invent new ideas here or reveal some newly discovered science - I am simply letting you realize that you are working for yourself and that means that you are the only one who is going to do the planning and also take the action steps.

Success in business is in implementing action and dedicating yourself to your business. You have measured your days and chalked down your hours. You have also gone ahead to plan everything and now we need to talk about making sure that taking the necessary action to reach our goals. It is the time to act.

There are a few things I want to focus on in this chapter;

1. **Procrastination**. I don't see procrastination as a habit; Instead, I see it as a comfort zone we get into. Some people say, 'I work best under pressure' or 'I always deliver on time but I work last minute'. All these are signs of procrastination. We have to take an action today. In Hindi there is a saying that goes thus, 'Whatever you are

supposed to do tomorrow, you have to do it today, and whatever you are supposed to do today, you have to do it now.' It basically means that the power is in now. You've got to take the action step now. So the question is how to overcome your procrastination.

Here's how.

a. If you have made your plans, they will motivate you. If you have not planned well enough it means that when you wake up in the morning you have no idea whatsoever on what you are supposed to do, and that is why you procrastinate. The reason we chalk down our hours is so that it motivates us and we know what we are supposed to do. When I get up, I don't want to think about what next. That's why we did amazing jobs when we worked for others; our work was planned, our calendars made, appointments were made and we simply had to go and deliver them.

So far in this book, you have made plans for yourself and this is the time for you to deliver and only you can do this. Anything and everything you do today will pay you later, so get over procrastination.

b. If you feel that you can't get over it without some help, well go read some books written on the subject. There are great books written on procrastination, books like 'The 12 week Year', which is an amazing book that tells about how you can do so much in 12 weeks than in a year, there are others about getting organized too.

Go do your research and find out books which will help you and motivate you. Use online YouTube videos to learn about how to overcome procrastinating. Get all the help you can. I did all of that – I read books and I searched for solutions, but the little secret is that it is you. It is you who is getting in the way of your own success.

Every time you procrastinate, you are putting yourself, your success, your business behind and getting those small pleasures instead. The pleasures of watching that movie, pleasures of watching TV, pleasures of taking an extra nap etc., whatever pleasure it is, it is short-lived.

So permit me to contradict myself by saying that when it comes to the subject of procrastination, you don't need to read a lot of books, trust me on this - I have read a lot of them.

I used to love doing research, you know, I'd pick up like ten books all talking about the same thing, always looking to find the best, until one day I realized what exactly it was that I was looking for; an easy way out.

The reason I read ten books and not go with even the first one is that I was looking for an easy way out. With each book I read, I was looking for something a little simpler to do, but there is nothing simple if you want success. You have to get up and do it, it is as simple as that, just get up and do it now.

c. If you are procrastinating, it is because you are not investing in yourself, so you have to talk to yourself and say, 'I invest in myself, and I am going to do everything I can to make my brand work.' Create affirmations for yourself, and post them on places where you can see them once you wake up, like your bathroom mirror so you see them when you are brushing and they serve as a reminder for you to take an action step now and not while away your time, sitting and reading the newspaper for an extra hour just because you don't have an appointment for that time. Use that time.

You have to stop procrastinating. Every time you procrastinate, I want you to remember that this is you getting in the way of your own success.

2. **Face Your Fears**. Most times, the thing that gets in our way when we are not procrastinating is our fears. Small, tiny fears. Fears like,

'what will people say?' when it comes to social media, or when it comes to stepping out, fears of 'how I look' so you don't try to meet more people. You may feel that you are not great at communicating, so you try to avoid events where you have to socialize and find new people for your business. These are small but they are fears and you do have to face them.

In 2017, I made a deal with myself which helped me a lot; every month I'd do at least one thing which doesn't naturally fall in my comfort zone. I'd do something that would challenge me and would force me to let go of certain fears and it worked. In twelve months, I did 12 different things and 2018 was a lot smoother because it changed me, making me more confident and comfortable in my own skin.

It doesn't matter what gender you are, we all have our fears. We all have challenges, we all have notions we have about ourselves because while we are told not to judge others we forget that we judge ourselves to a great extent and each judgment we place on ourselves is a new wall, a wall which stands between us and our success. So face your fears.

If you don't know what your fears are, next time you find yourself avoiding doing something, next time you feel yourself looking for an easy way out, go ahead and do it, not just because it is required, but because it is necessary that you break your own fears.

So, take the action step of breaking your fears by trying one new thing every fifteen days, things that you are not comfortable doing, it could be anything. For instance, it could be that you don't like taking a walk in the evening because you feel it is tasking to see certain people and getting into conversations and you hate conversations. So to avoid conversations you may not go for a walk.

We always have a cascading effect; because we don't like certain things as they would lead us to what we are scared of. Face your fears; ask yourself what you are really scared of, make a list of it and start ticking them off. You don't necessarily have to go bungee jumping or skydiving, although as the author of this book, I will be very happy if this book challenges you to take that step.

Realize that the ways to face these fears don't have to be expensive, just do things within your control. If, for instance, you are scared of social events, attend a few. Remember that if you were working for someone else, you would have done it, so go ahead and do those things.

Face your fears now. Eat that frog now.

3. **Try New Things**. Doing the same thing over and over again is monotonous and tends towards boredom. Although we like to live a principled and planned life, to a great extent we don't like doing the same thing every day. We don't like eating the same meal every day, and we don't like dressing the same way every day. We like change. Try some new things. If you have been doing your business in a particular fashion for a long time, change your ways, edit a few things, try new things not just for your business but for yourself as well.

   'I work for me' - so everything you do will be towards your own progress and success. So, go ahead, try new things for yourself and for your business.

4. **Just Do It**. I know we have spoken about procrastination as the first point, but that was about getting out of your comfort zone. The fourth point is about just doing it. You may not like a routine, or doing certain things, but if they are requirements of what is needed for your success, just do it.

   Sometimes it is about starting off and after the first minute of unhappiness or displeasure, you will get into the flow and your body will get used to it and you will find that you like the activities that you do. When I say just do it, I am talking about little things, things like planning. Every night you are supposed to make a plan for the next day, so sit down and make the plan.

There will be times when you feel lazy, there will be times when you don't like it, but just do it because it will make your next day a lot smoother and when you get up you know what you need to do. If you don't plan, you get into the vicious cycle of falling into procrastination or delayed thinking and saying things like 'I don't know what to do today'.

If you just do what you need to, things fall into place and you find that you have fewer things to worry about.

Just do it now.

5. **Stay Healthy**. Stay healthy, stay mindful. When talking about business, talk about your health too. Your health is like your finance. If your company is going to succeed, you need the basic finance to be put in place. When it comes to you working for yourself, your finance is your health. It is your treasure and you have to preserve it. You have to have a disciplined life, live healthily and eat healthy. You are not doing this for anyone else but for yourself and for your own success. Be mindful, be aware of what you do, and why you do them.

   Take healthy steps, get mindful now.

6. **Meditate**. Meditate often. I know meditation may not be something you really like. I didn't like the thought of meditating. I didn't like the fact that I had to sit in one place and stay idle, doing nothing. At least that was what came to my mind when I thought of meditation. Eventually though, I met some gurus who told me that I didn't have to sit at a place to meditate, instead, I should do something which I really enjoy and get lost in it and that could be my meditation.

I realize that at the initial stage, for so many years, I cooked because I loved cooking and I got lost in it. Every time I cooked, I got some amazing ideas and that is what meditation was for me. Today though, I know that sitting down for a while and centering in on myself and bringing my entire awareness to myself helped me grow, it helped me have a vision and it helped me see through things.

Meditate, start with baby steps, you don't have to begin by meditating every day. You can start with once a week or once in fifteen days or anytime you remember but make sure you meditate as it helps you. It doesn't matter what gender or age you are, just practice it and put it in your action plan

Remember this chapter is all about taking action – so while you've got to take the action, you've got to pause for a while. Meditation is that pause for you. In your life, as you have many things to do continuously, meditation would give you that pause and breath that is required.

You don't have to meditate now, but make an appointment with yourself for meditation ... or you could just do it now.

7. **Keep Upgrading Yourself**. What I mean by this , is for you to learn something new every year. See if you are updated with the latest technology and the latest knowledge or news about your business. Keep learning, keep upgrading.

About 8 or 9 years ago, I realized that anytime I needed to learn something new to upgrade myself, I felt it was a burden and didn't usually have enough savings for my own learning, so one thing I now do which has helped me for so many years is to put aside 10 to 20% of my income so that when I want to learn that new skill for the year, I am financially strong and don't have to depend on anyone or compromise on my holidays or fun time or other luxuries. It has helped me.

You can think of different ways to do it but keep upgrading yourself. The longer you stay as a learner, the more quickly you succeed in your path of life. If you observe people who are always ready to learn and upgrade themselves, you find that they are always, absolutely successful.

Many still feel that technology is a burden. I am not talking about technology, I am not talking about you taking computer classes, I am not talking about you learning how to use the iPad or how to programme if you are not a programmer - I am talking about you doing something for yourself, something to improve yourself.

If you are a writer, do something for yourself where you meet other writers. If you are a jewelry designer, go for a new course where you can learn some new technology when it comes to designing jewelry. If you are a mechanical engineer who has spent all his life working for others and is now starting his own business, go ahead and learn any new knowledge you need to have so that you are upgraded. It makes you more knowledgeable and approachable and it also helps you build trust in people.

Keep upgrading yourself. Do it because it is an investment, and you investing in yourself is the best investment ever.

Get upgraded now.

When we talk about now being the time we are talking about you getting up and taking action right now. Let me repeat what I said earlier, anytime you procrastinate and say, 'I will do it later,' you are delaying your own progress, you are getting in your own way. You know what should be done to the barriers to your success; kill them because you don't want to break or limit yourself, so go ahead, take that action step and do what you need to do now.

Live up to your clock, live up to your plans, and follow the role that you have given yourself.

Now is the time. Take action now.

"D"
DON'T STOP

D on't stop; keep that ball rolling.
It is usually said that success is like a snowball, it takes momentum to build, and the more you roll in the right direction, the bigger it gets. Any business will survive when you make it last. To make it last, you have to keep the ball rolling. Life is like a rollercoaster but it is worth it all, you just have to set your intentions and stick to it. That is how you keep the ball rolling, by sticking to it, by not stopping.

Everything discussed in previous chapters is to make you realize and understand that you are capable and that you are enough. That is why the book is called 'I Work for Me'. You are enough as long as you are doing what is required and you keep doing it; you stick to it like clockwork or a cycle and you repeat your actions. Of course, you change some actions depending on the results but taking your action steps and keeping to them is what is required.

Don't stop.

Oliver Herford also said that a rolling stone gathers no moss but it obtains a certain polish, and that polish is nothing but you becoming so much better in everything you do. The Universe is always giving.

Everything and anything grows if you are putting your attention on it. There is no one giant step that does it all; it takes little steps to help you cross the journey, so take those action steps every day.

Keep that ball rolling by keeping yourself upgraded at every opportunity. Realize that it is all about you fulfilling your promises and it is about you making sure that you are doing what is required of you. It is never too late for you to become who you might have been. Let this day be the day you release yourself from the imprisonment of past grudges and anger, simplify your life, let go of the poisonous past and live abundantly, live beautifully, live presently and live today.

Let today be the day you set yourself free.

Here are a few tips on how to keep that ball rolling;

1. **Say Yes**. While I have talked about investing in yourself, you must realize that working for yourself is dynamic and fluid and at best a 'work in progress'. Work is part of what you do continually to succeed in life, and that requires you to be willing to bide time or to have that staying power. Say Yes to embrace the energy and effort, regardless of the outcome. Otherwise your efforts are going to be a waste and you find yourself always starting over in new endeavors or businesses, always coming to the same point and never getting to the point where you reap results from your efforts because you quit too soon.

So, say yes, as it allows things to happen at different stages. In business, not everything will go your way. 'Yes' usually turns into 'Yes, but...' while you are saying 'yes', it is sometimes backed with 'however,...' and many other things. Remember that saying yes allows for a more open and positive approach to things, even to disagreements and conflicts. Saying yes creates a simple but beautiful environment for you to succeed; instead of saying no and stopping the flow halfway or before you get your results. Don't stop saying yes.

2. **Keep Yourself Occupied**. Do not allow past failures to define your future path. Successes don't come easily and when you work for

you, you discover a lot of things about yourself. You learn and unlearn a lot of things about yourself too, as well as about the people around you and how the world operates.

When you work for someone else, the world operates in a different way, but when you work for you, when you have your own company, the world changes. When you work for yourself you are not only the service provider, you are also the decision maker, you are also the sales creator, you are also someone looking to make profits, so your world changes and the way you see and move through the world changes. As is said, the road looks different when you are on the driver's seat.

Will you have failures? Yes, of course, you will have failures, but at that point choose to remember what you have learnt out of the experience and move on. What is going to help you, is for you not to give up but take the failure with a pinch of salt and move on. Don't stop.

3. **Intention Setting**. I know we did this in a previous chapter, but I am going to refresh your **memory** by repeating it now. Each time you put effort into your company, every time you invest into your brand, I want you to get to it only with thoughts of succeeding at it. Failure is evident, if you are not successful, you will fail. It's that simple. You don't have to jump into something with the thought that it is okay to fail.

Remove that thought.

Instead, get into it saying, 'I'm putting in 100% or 200% and let's see where it takes me. The worst is that I will learn out of this and I will know what not to do'. So, change your approach. How we look at success and failure, how we perceive success and failure is important, how we calculate our gains and losses is important in helping us keep that ball rolling.

Take control of your own life by keeping yourself occupied with successful thoughts.

Don't stop the right intention settings; don't stop the successful thoughts flowing.

4. **Have a Winning Attitude**. Wherever you are right now, you didn't get there without failure at least once, be it in relationships, in work, or in studies, it could be in anything, but we have all had our share of failures. What has kept you going, what is going to keep you going is a positive, winning attitude.

   You have to ask yourself these questions;

- Do you believe that working for yourself will help you attain and achieve your long-term goals?
- Do you believe that by doing this you are going to be a better person?
- Do you believe that the experience is going to be a positive one?
   If you answered no to any of the above questions, then you need to work on your positive attitude.

   I gave tips to having a positive attitude at the start of this book, and I am going to repeat them.

   a. ***Start Your Day Right***. Start each day in the right direction by choosing to wake up with a smile. Having a good breakfast is your first positive foundation for the day. Always remind yourself that life is short and you are going to make the most of it each and every day. Not only will this leave you with a positive attitude, it would also help you stay alert and focused while you work for yourself.

   b. ***Choose the Right Words***. When you define or describe your work, ensure you choose the right words. The words you use have an impact on whether you give off a positive or a negative attitude. Engage in positive conversations daily, say to yourself, 'I have a positive attitude towards my business, I am capable of finding my own solution, I can and I will be successful, I can do it'. Such affirmations help you build the right, positive mindset.

One thing I learnt in coaching is that each and every person is whole and complete and capable of finding their own solutions. Likewise you are whole and complete and capable of finding your own solutions, and capable of being successful - it's all in you.

So what do you tell yourself when you get up? There are some preconceived notions which you put in your mind and some which have come from you through your association with others. .

Words like;

"He's a good communicator but I don't think he sells good."

Or

"He cannot sell a single thing to anyone."

People make comments about you and you make them a reality by living them. So, change your words. As I said, you are whole and complete and are capable of finding your own solutions.

Be wise, choose the right words for yourself, always. Don't stop.

c. **_Keep Positive Company_**. You probably have in your association, friends and family who have a negative attitude. You know, those who don't support you most of the times and you are very careful when you talk to them. If you have such friends who have a negative attitude about school, or have a negative attitude towards your business, or who have a negative attitude and believe that the chances of you being successful or doing good is slim, then it's time you make sure that you get and keep the right company. You may want to consider friends who will encourage you, support and motivate you to have a positive attitude.

There was a beautiful article written by my coach, "*Drainers versus Energizers*". Make a rundown of your life and discover those who energize you and help you move forward in life. Discover also, those who can take you ten steps backward in life with a single comment, draining your energy; those people who when you sit with them for just a few minutes, you wonder when the discussion will be over; you need to avoid such people and you need to make a change.

Explore organizations, explore book clubs and other places like gyms. Explore these places for people with positive attitude and influence, people who are encouraging about your business and about you working for yourself. Such people exist, go search them out.

Don't stop searching out positive company.

d.   **Be Thankful**. Once in a while, take an inventory of your life and appreciate what you have; family, friends, work, ideas, food, education, experience etc. All these are things to be thankful for. No matter how difficult life gets, there are always things, for which we can be thankful for. This gratefulness can have a profound impact on your attitude towards your business and other aspects of your life.

Let me tell you a recent experience which you may not be able to relate with, but it is important that I share this.

My first book, 'Twenty Beautiful Women', was about my life story and what I went through. In the book, although I knew I had achieved a lot, I felt that life was really hard.

This book was written about two years ago.

Just a few days ago, I was watching a movie called 'Mom'. It is an Indian movie about a girl who got raped. It may sound exaggerated, but while I was watching the movie, which started off showing what the girl had; a father who loved her, a mother who was ready to love her although she didn't want anything to do with her mom. She had a cute little sister, and everything that she needed like money, education, comfort etc. I was mumbling at how she had everything and how lucky she was, until the story changed.

She got raped in a very safe environment. Not an unsafe environment where the struggles are obvious, but in a safe environment. This had me thinking to myself about how I keep complaining of where I was born and the struggles I went through, but how there were still many things I should be grateful for.

I was saved. I lived in a really bad neighborhood, and still didn't experience many bad things that could have happened. Did I have many things to be thankful for? Yes. Instead of complaining about the neighborhood, I could have been grateful for being saved and safe every day of my life. I slept in my own bed, absolutely safe, with my parents around me, every single day of my life as a child. I have things to be grateful for, and I had to make the choice to look at things in a different way.

All I am trying to say here is that you should be thankful. Every day, you will have 20 or maybe 40 things to complain about, but trust me you'll always have hundreds of things to be grateful for and be thankful for and feel blessed for. That is one reason I love the song, 'Count your blessings'. Count your blessings, count them one by one. God will always shower you with His blessings.

I don't know if you believe in God or not, but I do. I believe in the Universe, I believe in a power that is greater than me and I know that if I am grateful for everything that I have, I will have it in multiples, as I said, everything that you focus on expands.

Don't stop being thankful.

e. **_Avoid Negative Triggers_**. While in business, working for ourselves, feelings of being upset, frustration and anger are things that we sometimes allow ourselves to get accustomed to. Be conscious of what situations make you upset or frustrated. When you can identify these situations, you can successfully take steps to avoid them. Do this for yourself.

If it is a friend who is confrontational, avoid such a friend. If it is a situation which causes you a high level of stress, avoid the situation. If it is an unavoidable situation, make plans to approach it with a positive attitude. Decide and talk yourself into not allowing it to affect you negatively, then try to make the best of it.

The brain is a smart organ. Once we identify the negative triggers, we find out that we begin to respond differently instead of reacting to these situations. Remember, as I said earlier, every person is whole and complete and you will find your own solutions, just be aware of these situations.

Don't stop being aware. Avoid negative triggers.

f.   ***Learn to Accept Feedback***. You may be of the opinion that you have an absolutely great and positive attitude towards life and your business, but others may not perceive it the same way. So ask people you trust to give you feedback and try to listen with an open mind to what they say.

When I was a trainer, I made sure to speak about being open to feedback because I realized over a period of time that people usually think that they know anything and everything about themselves and have no idea how the world sees them. That is where Johari's Window comes in. If you don't know what that is, you can use Google to find out, or watch YouTube videos to know what Johari's Window means.

You don't have to listen to everyone's feedback, but be open to listening to feedback. You also don't have to listen and take action immediately or do what others are telling you to do. What you have to do is listen to what they have to say, take time and analyze it and if there is evidence, if there is an iota of truth, go ahead and make the necessary change.

You are not working for someone else, you are not making the change as a favor for someone else, you are doing this for yourself and that is one way your positive attitude can truly be positive. People may say things which are difficult to accept but many times the best changes in our lives come from constructive criticisms.

So, learn to accept feedback to keep the ball rolling.

g. **Make the Change.** If you get to realize or recognize that your attitude is negatively affecting your success, it is time to take action and divorce it. Refuse to be dragged down and kept low by a negative attitude. It is not okay to go ahead with the flow and keep saying 'This is how I am, I am not going to change myself…' if you know that it is acting as a barrier, it has to go. It may be the most difficult thing to do, but trust that it is worth it.

I know this because I somehow grew up with the belief and thought that I am not a great sales person and I can never sell anything. I believed I was a great customer service personnel. I understood people and their needs and I was ready to deliver what they needed, but I couldn't tell someone to please buy my services because I didn't see why anyone should buy my services. So I believed I was not a sales person at all.

Soon, however, I realized I was the one acting as my own barrier. If I was so good at understanding what the customers needed, and I knew how to give them the required service and made sure that it was effective, then I am the one who knows what the client needs and selling is something I should also be doing, but I wasn't.

So I made the necessary change.

Your success in your work, in your business and in your life, depends in part on your attitude. A strong and positive attitude creates more miracles than any other thing. Life is 10% how you make it and 90% how you take it.

Don't stop making the necessary changes.

So, work on your attitude, keep that ball rolling by giving yourself 100%. Don't stop giving 100%. Having the right attitude is the best business tool you'll ever have. Keep improving on your attitude. Your attitude is your choice, and a positive attitude says a lot about you.

A positive attitude says you believe you can succeed. It is not a guarantee of success, but it is a pillow on which your success can be achieved. People tend to trust people with positive attitudes; people are drawn to those with positive attitudes because they are confident that the person will make rational and reasonable decisions.

There are many advantages and gifts that come with having a positive attitude. A positive attitude helps you in rough situations. There are times when your honor, credibility, knowledge and everything will be tested and challenged. In such situations, your positive attitude will help keep the ball rolling and keep the confidence going and keep you competent enough to do your job and stay working for yourself.

THE FIRST EVER BOOK REVIEW *BY* AMY BLOUSTINE

Snehal acknowledges, at the outset, that we are all at different places in our career path as entrepreneurs or solopreneurs. We all have our paths to create, and we all need help along the way, whether we ask for it or not.

She starts with laying out sensible steps for anyone starting a business and even has great reminders for those who have been in business for a long time. It's not a one – size – fits - all approach; instead it's a take-what – works-for-you one.

This book resonates with many parts of our lives, professionally and personally and I think it's a holistic approach focusing on the mind, body, and soul while helping us set the intention of staying true to ourselves and finding a version that works best for us.

I Work for Me sets you on a course of self-exploration, a new way of thinking and exploring your own life and business and Snehal asks very poignant questions along the way that gets you to think in a way you might not have or wanted to otherwise. I like that this is thought-provoking and an actionable handbook with such valuable tools, resources, and tips that are practical, attainable and realistic for everyone.

Snehal's words and thoughts give you permission to be vulnerable, be a superhero, and be your most authentic self. I have had the opportunity of working with her on another book project, and I can't praise her enough for her support, knowledge, and inspiration. It's my own experience that gives me the privilege to review this book, in all honesty. She has your best interest at heart when sharing the steps and wisdom of building a business. She knows how to connect with people; she helps you find your inner strength and helps you get in touch with your vision. Her words, written or spoken will bring you happiness, light, and fantastic energy into your life.

There are so many takeaways from this book, but most of all, I like the simplistic approach, and I appreciate her honesty, her story, and her truth, which we can relate to in one way or another. I found myself nodding in agreement as I read through the book. Making notes on the side about how I had gone through what she was writing about and the examples that she refers to felt like she was talking about my life.

Most of all, this book gives you hope that you are on the right path, that you don't have to do it alone, that you have your story and your journey to embark upon, and whatever version you choose, it is yours.

Amy Bloustine, ACC, M.Ed.

Certified Life and Career Coach, Trained Recovery Coach, President of the Board of Directors for the New York City International Coach Federation Chapter.

LinkedIn - https://www.linkedin.com/in/abloustine/

A LITTLE NOTE
FROM THE AUTHOR

I hope this book is going to help you to consciously and deliberately make yourself successful. **I Work for Me** is my baby project and I have practically put down everything that is making me successful. I call myself successful because **I.M.B.R.A.N.D**, looking at where I started to where I am today, I know I am successful.

I feel grateful for all those messages and emails I keep getting every day. My day starts with at least a request saying, 'Snehal I saw your post and felt I should connect with you', and things like these make me happy. This is what I call success because I have people across the globe approaching me; that's how I define success.

You are free to decide on your own definition of success and you are free to choose your own way of experiences. I can keep talking about positive attitude and other things, but I need you to remember that each day we have the power to choose the attitude we take into the day. By choosing to be positive, we attract more positive experiences our way and the same goes with negative experiences.

We work with the power of the Universe and it is in sync with our energies and our frequencies and our subconscious and our soul. Naturally, if everything is synced with the universe it will grow. That is the normal way of things.

So, be strengthened, be empowered, love yourself, do what is right and work for you because that is the biggest gift you can give yourself.

Tell yourself, IMBRAND and be yourself. For we are God's masterpiece (Ephesians 2:10)

Live your life successfully, work for you.

Let me know how this book has helped you. If there is something more you would like to know, reach me via email at snehal@snehalrsingh.com or book an appointment with me on my website – www.mindspiritworks.com

Connect with me, I would love to reply your emails and help more.

Love and Light,

Snehal R. Singh

Made in the USA
Columbia, SC
02 May 2019